DINO-WHY?

THE DINOSAUR QUESTION & ANSWER BOOK

Sylvia Funston

MAPLE
TREE
PRESS

Maple Tree Press Inc.
51 Front Street East, Suite 200, Toronto, Ontario M5E 1B3
www.mapletreepress.com

2008 edition © Maple Tree Press
This book contains material that previously appeared in *The Dinosaur Question and Answer Book,* © 1992.
All material has been revised and updated for this edition.

Distributed in Canada by Raincoast Books
9050 Shaughnessy Street, Vancouver, British Columbia V6P 6E5

Distributed in the United States by Publishers Group West
1700 Fourth Street, Berkeley, California 94710

Acknowledgments
The author and publisher extend their thanks to the scientists and staff affiliated with the Ex Terra Foundation, and especially to Dr. Philip Currie, Dr. Dale Russell and John Acorn, whose help and advice on the first edition of this book was invaluable.

Cataloguing in Publication Data
Funston, Sylvia
    Dino–why? : the dinosaur question and answer book / Sylvia Funston. — Updated and rev. ed.

Includes index.
ISBN 978-1-897349-24-3 (bound)   ISBN 978-1-897349-25-0 (pbk.)

    1. Dinosaurs—Miscellanea—Juvenile literature. I. Title.

QE861.5.F86 2008   j567.9   C2007-906068-4

Library of Congress Control Number: 2007939082

Design: Julia Naimska and Claudia Dávila
Design concept: Julie Colantonio
Art direction: Julia Naimska and Claudia Dávila
Front cover illustration: *Allosaurus Fragilis,* with permission of the Royal Ontario Museum © ROM
Back cover illustration: Graeme Walker

We acknowledge the financial support of the Canada Council for the Arts, the Ontario Arts Council, the Government of Canada through the Book Publishing Industry Development Program (BPIDP), and the Government of Ontario through the Ontario Media Development Corporation's Book Initiative for our publishing activities.

ONTARIO ARTS COUNCIL
CONSEIL DES ARTS DE L'ONTARIO

In the field of paleontology new discoveries are constantly being made and theories modified. The information contained in *Dino–Why?* is believed by experts at the time of printing to be correct.

Printed in China

A   B   C   D   E   F

INTRODUCTION

If you could ask just one question about dinosaurs what would it be? That's a tough one, isn't it? There are so many fascinating facts to discover about some of the most amazing animals that ever walked on this planet.

But you can relax. You don't have to rack your brains for that perfect question because we've done all the hard work for you. We've read and thought very carefully about questions already asked by kids just like you—11,000 questions to be precise.

The really hard part was choosing the ones that this book will answer. You'll find some obvious and some not-so-obvious questions, as well as questions that will make you think about dinosaurs in new and exciting ways. And some questions even had dinosaur experts scratching their heads in wonder. We hope you have as much fun finding out the answers as we did.

ARE YOU A DINO-BUFF?

Before you jump into big questions about dinosaurs, find out how much you already know about them. This quiz will reveal your true Dino-Buff rating.

1. What is a dinosaur?

a. A lizard with a crazy walk.
b. A special type of land reptile that lived millions of years ago in the late Triassic, the Jurassic and the Cretaceous periods.
c. A long-legged crocodile.

2. Where did dinosaurs come from?

a. They arrived on a spaceship.
b. They turned overnight from lizards into dinosaurs.
c. They evolved gradually from a group of ancient reptiles called thecodonts.

3. Where did dinosaurs live?

a. In many different environments—ranging from swamps to forests to deserts—on every continent on Earth.
b. In big caves.
c. On the slopes of volcanoes.

4. When did dinosaurs live?

a. They didn't—they're a myth.
b. The first true dinosaur appeared about 215 million years ago. Dinosaurs lived on Earth for the next 150 million years.
c. Sometime between the invention of the wheel and the first video game.

5. Did some dinosaurs live in the sea?

a. Some tried, but the salt hurt their eyes too much.
b. No, dinosaurs never lived in the sea.
c. Yes, but the waves made them seasick.

6. Were the flying pterosaurs a type of dinosaur?

a. Yes, the type that was not afraid of heights.
b. No, they were a type of adventurous flying fish.
c. No, they were a special type of reptile that flew.

7. Are dinosaurs related to crocodiles?

a. No, their closest relatives are bumblebees.
b. No, they're second cousins to jellyfish.
c. Yes, they're distantly related.

11. If you were a paleontologist, what would you study?

a. Ancient life on Earth.
b. Ancient life on other planets.
c. Ancient life in other galaxies.

8. What other kinds of animals were alive during dinosaur times?

a. There were many other kinds of animals also living then, including the ancestors of every animal on Earth today.
b. With all those dinosaurs galumphing around, there was no room for other animals.
c. Only tree-dwelling animals that were masters of disguise.

10. Did all the different kinds of dinosaurs live at the same time?

a. Yes, and it got very crowded.
b. No, dinosaur species evolved and became extinct throughout the entire 150-million-year period that they were on Earth.
c. Yes, and they had terrible family squabbles.

12. What does the word *dinosaur* mean?

a. Noisy, bad-tempered beast.
b. Hungry monster.
c. Terrible lizard.

9. What were the two main groups of dinosaurs called?

a. Bird-hipped and lizard-hipped.
b. Bird-lipped and lizard-lipped.
c. Bird-footed and lizard-footed.

Dino-score

Give yourself a point for each correct answer. (Answers: page 64.)

0–4 Room for improvement. Better make that room enough for *Seismosaurus*.

5–8 You're on the right track. Careful you don't fall into a huge footprint left by *Mamenchisaurus*.

9–12 What a Dino-Buff! You'd know exactly what to do if you were being chased by *Troodon*. Well, wouldn't you?

5

WHY ARE NAMES OF DINOSAURS SO COMPLICATED?

 hy would scientists want to give any self-respecting dinosaur as complex a name as *Micropachycephalosaurus hongtuyanensis*? Because that name describes it perfectly.

Take the first word. *Micro, pachy, cephalo* and *saurus* are Greek words meaning "small thick-headed reptile." Add to this the second word, which describes the red rock formation where the dinosaur was found. Then the entire name means "the small, thick-headed reptile from the place with red rocks," which is in Laiyang, Shandong, in China. Whew! What could be clearer than that?

How would you say *Micropachycephalosaurus* in Russian, Chinese or French? Exactly the same way. Scientists all over the world use the same Greek or Latin names to describe plants and animals. *Micropachycephalosaurus* was named in 1978 by Dong Zhiming, shown below working on a stegosaur backbone.

WERE THERE MANY TYPES OF DINOSAURS?

magine one species of dinosaur separating into two groups that live in different places. Over a million or so years, the two groups can change so much that they evolve into two different species. If this sort of split happens regularly, after 150 million years you should have billions of species of dinosaurs. Yet, because different species of dinosaurs became extinct over the years, there were probably no more than a few hundred thousand species.

Of course, no one knows how many new dinosaur species are still buried. Dinosaur remains have been found at more than 1000 locations world-wide. Today, dinosaur hunters are just as likely to go to Africa, South America, Antarctica or Siberia as they are to visit the better-known bone beds in Europe, North America and China.

Dinosaur Jumble

Whoops! Somebody mixed up the meaning of these dinosaur terms. Can you unscramble them?

tri	foot
dino	big
mega	tyrant
pod	tooth
micro	reptile
tyranno	terrible
donto	small
saur	three

Answers: page 64. For more about dinosaur words, check the glossary on page 60.

HOW DO YOU KNOW **WHERE** TO LOOK FOR DINOSAURS?

Paleontologists look on geology maps for areas of sedimentary rocks, formed out of layers of mud, sand or gravel. They look for rocks the same age as dinosaurs (between 215 million and 65 million years old). And for exposed sedimentary rocks where weather or water erosion has done some of the hard work of digging for them. With luck, they might even find fossils sticking out of the ground. This type of erosion is often found in rocky outcrops in places such as the Gobi Desert in Mongolia (large photo), the Sahara, Australia's outback or North America's badlands. The Canadian Arctic (inset photo), which once had a tropical climate, is another dinosaur bone bed.

WHY DID DINOSAURS GET BURIED?

 ossils are mistakes of nature's recycling system. Dead animals are meant to be eaten or decomposed by millions of bacteria and other tiny organisms. But fossils are the remains of animals that were buried before they had a chance to decompose. Landslides engulfed some, silt quickly deposited on river bottoms covered others. And desert sandstorms entombed still others, like these 12 young *Pinacosaurus* whose fossils were discovered 80 million years later in the Gobi Desert.

Scientists used sonar (a sound version of radar) to take "sound pictures" of *Seismosaurus*, an immense sauropod, while it was still in the ground.

HOW DO YOU GET DINOSAUR BONES OUT OF THE ROCK?

 Tyrannosaurus rex was dug out of a rockface in Crowsnest Pass, Alberta, with jackhammers, and dynamite might be the only solution for removing tons of extra-hard overlying rock. But there are other, less noisy ways of getting dinosaur bones out of rock. If you're fortunate enough to find small fossils in limestone, you can usually chisel out a chunk of fossil-bearing rock then soak it in a weak acid bath in the laboratory. The acid eats away the limestone, leaving behind the fossils.

Do Dinosaur Hunters Use Lasers?

f a laser ever exists that can zap away tons of rock without damaging fossil bones trapped inside, paleontologists will rush to buy it. What does exist is lidar, a laser version of radar, that can take multiple 3D snapshots of bones as they're being dug up. Excavators can seldom photograph an entire skeleton because each bone must be wrapped quickly to avoid damage from exposure to the air. Sorting through hundreds of photos of individual bones to assemble a picture of the animal is difficult and tedious. With lidar all you have to do is input its scans into a computer. A software program creates a 3D image of the complete dinosaur, as well as a 3D map of the environment in which it was found.

▲ Sometimes you've got to blast through tons of rock to get at well-buried dinosaurs.

▼ Here is an artist's impression of the 12 young *Pinacosaurus* as blowing sand overcomes them.

9

WHAT WOULD YOU TAKE ON A DINOSAUR HUNT?

 part from your cell phone and the number of a helicopter-delivery pizza parlor, here is some equipment that would come in handy. Can you match up the tools with the descriptions of how they're used?

▲ **Gently does it! A scalpel is the perfect tool for scraping soft sandstone rock from the skull of this young _Pinacosaurus_ found in the Gobi Desert.**

burlap

brush

rope and pulleys

1. Used to measure fossils and distances between them while they are in the ground.

2. Used to remove large amounts of hard rock above or around the fossil, but not right next to the fossil.

3. Used to record each step in the process of taking a fossil out of the ground. It is important for scientists to know how the bones were lying and what kind of rock surrounded them.

4. Used to remove sand and dust from the fossil, once you have removed most of the rock.

5. Used to strengthen the fossil, so it doesn't crumble when you take it out of the ground.

6. Used to examine small fossils, such as teeth and scales.

7. Used like a miniature jackhammer to remove small amounts of hard rock from the fossils.

8. Coated with plaster of paris to make "jackets" to protect large or fragile fossils while they are transported to the laboratory.

9. Used to remove small amounts of rock, to clear off layers of sediments, and as a climbing tool.

10. Used to lift heavy jacketed fossils. Sometimes a helicopter has to lift extra-large jacketed fossils out of rough terrain.

Answers: page 64.

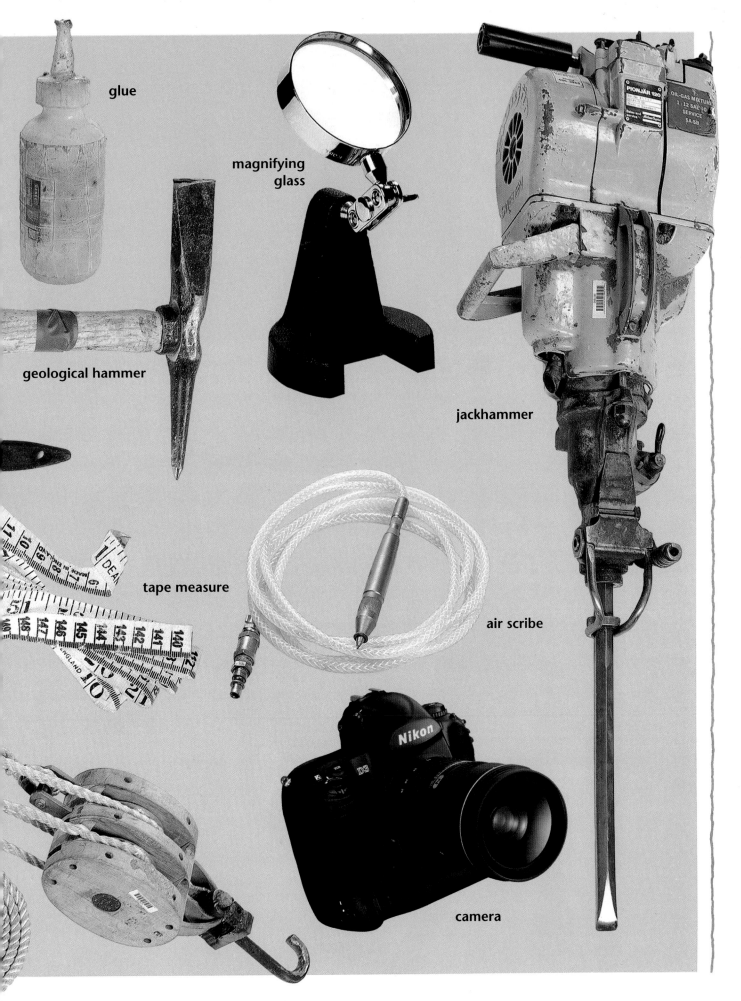

glue

magnifying glass

geological hammer

jackhammer

tape measure

air scribe

camera

11

HOW DO SCIENTISTS KNOW SO MUCH ABOUT DINOSAURS?

 Paleontologists use computers and technology from industry, medicine and other sciences to unlock dinosaur secrets from fossils. British paleontologist Angela Milner took an *Archaeopteryx* skull all the way to Texas because a scientist there had a computed tomography (CT) scanner powerful enough to see through bone and rock and tell the difference between them. *Archaeopteryx* was a small, meat-eating dinosaur with the wings and feathers of a modern bird. But did it have a dino-brain or a bird-brain? Many hours of scanning and computer analysis produced the answer: the skull would have housed the brain of a modern bird, fully equipped for flight. Archae would have chirped, not roared.

A fossilized bone is being prepared in a laboratory. A fine-tipped drill is used to remove the fossil from the rock. It's slow, careful work, better done at the laboratory than out in the field.

Did male *Parasaurolophus* grow large, showy headgear to attract females? New ways of looking at evidence might reveal all one day.

HOW CAN YOU TELL IF A DINOSAUR IS MALE OR FEMALE?

The only foolproof way to identify a female dino is to find unlaid eggs inside her body (see page 16). Or so we thought...until paleontologist Mary Schweitzer took a really close look at the inside of a thigh bone belonging to a 68-million-year-old tyrannosaur named *B-rex*. To her amazement, Mary saw a bony structure usually found only in female birds. It's a storehouse for calcium, which birds use to make eggshells. *B-rex* was really Betty-rex.

A CT scan of a *Parasaurolophus* skull revealed previously unknown chambers and tubes in its crest. A computer program worked out their size and shape then produced the sound that the animal could have made using its crest as an amplifier. A voice from the past. Is that spooky, or what?

WHAT DO MICROSCOPES TELL YOU ABOUT DINOSAURS?

ifferent microscopes tell different stories. Polarizing light microscopes, for instance, reveal growth rings in bones. Those in T-rex bones show that this mighty theropod reached its gigantic size during a monster adolescent growth spurt. Between the ages of 14 and 18 a teen T-rex would have packed on 2 kg (over 4 lb.) a day (think of the growing pains!) before slowing down and reaching its adult weight— about the same as your average African elephant.

DO DINO-HUNTERS SHARE THEIR DISCOVERIES WITH EACH OTHER?

hey do. But one of the problems they have is how to let other scientists see their discoveries so they too can research them. Dinosaur bones are either too fragile or too big and heavy to travel. One solution is to use a hand-held laser scanner to produce 3D virtual replicas of bones in such fine detail that other scientists can study them on their computers without the risk of damaging the originals.

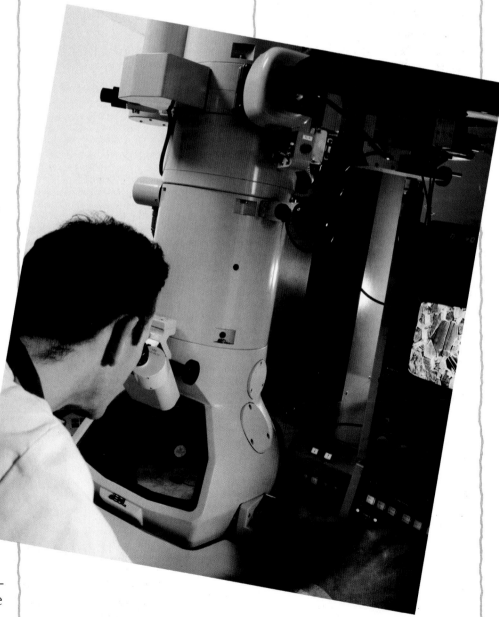

⚠ A laboratory technician looks into a scanning electron microscope (SEM), which uses an electron beam to obtain a 3D image of an object.

WHAT DO DINOSAUR BONES FEEL LIKE?

If you've ever eaten chicken wings or drumsticks, you know that bones are hard and smooth. They are also lightweight, because they are filled with air holes. But a 65-million-year-old dinosaur bone comes out of the ground a lot heavier than it was when it went in because it has fossilized. In this process, water full of dissolved minerals seeps into the bone, slowly turning it to stone. And stone weighs more than bone.

HOW DO BONES TELL YOU WHAT DINOSAURS LOOKED LIKE?

Bones are full of information if you know what to look for. Wherever a muscle attaches to a bone, for instance, you'll find a bump on the bone. (Compared with a weight lifter's bone bumps, yours will be positively puny.) Also, most animals with four limbs have the same types of bones in similar places. By studying how the skeletons and muscles of modern animals work, paleontologists can get a clear picture of what a living, moving dinosaur must have looked like. Scientists now know for certain what some small Chinese dinosaurs looked like because their shapes have been preserved by fine volcanic ash. Other dinosaur fossils found in the same place had well-preserved soft parts and body coverings.

▲ **Philip Currie from Alberta's Tyrrell Museum compares the length of his lower leg with that of a meat-eating, Gobi Desert theropod.**

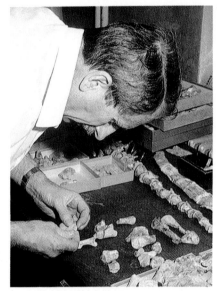

▲ **Canadian paleontologist Dale Russell sorts through some dinosaur bones looking for that perfect fit.**

HOW DO SCIENTISTS KNOW HOW TO PUT DINOSAUR SKELETONS TOGETHER CORRECTLY?

Dinosaur bones fit together in the same way as other animal skeletons, so it's not difficult to tell where each bone belongs. But sometimes bones from more than one dinosaur get mixed together. Then it's hard to tell how many backbones or ribs each animal should have. Or, a skeleton might be missing vital pieces. An *Apatosaurus* stood for years at the Carnegie Museum of Natural History, Pittsburgh, with the wrong head—until its own was discovered.

"Black Beauty" claw

"Black Beauty" toe bones

The bones of a *Tyrannosaurus rex* from Alberta turned black when magnesium compounds from groundwater seeped into them while they were being fossilized. Scientists dubbed the skeleton "Black Beauty."

◄ Recent studies suggest that sauropods such as *Mamenchisaurus* probably walked with their heads parallel to the ground. Though they might have lifted their heads to feed, a computer model of a sauropod raising its neck vertically, like the one here, showed that its neck bones collided with each other after being raised more than 4 m (13 ft.) above its shoulder. Sauropods might have been more comfortable browsing on riverside bushes, not high up in trees.

Mamenchisaurus skeleton

HOW CAN YOU TELL A BABY DINOSAUR FROM A VERY SMALL ADULT?

t can be very difficult. You can check if certain back and skull bones have fused together as they do in adults. But if these fused parts are missing? US paleontologist Jack Horner examines bone growth in bone slices under a special microscope. Then he takes CT scans of whole bones to create a 3D model of the animal. Software uses the bone growth information to calculate how the animal would grow, then digitally morphs the 3D model into its adult form. If it morphs into something bigger, the skeleton belongs to a youngster.

WHY DID HUGE DINOSAURS LAY SUCH SMALL EGGS?

ypacrosaurus was long enough that if you parked a school bus beside one, there wouldn't be much bus sticking out at either end! Yet the female laid eggs that were no bigger than large cantaloupes. Why didn't she lay bigger eggs?

There comes a point where you can't make an egg any bigger because the bigger the egg, the thicker its shell must be. A really thick shell would prevent oxygen from reaching the embryo inside. And hatchlings would need a hammer and chisel to break out! In the case of eggs, then, bigger isn't always better.

DID DINOSAURS LAY ALL THEIR EGGS AT ONCE LIKE CROCODILES DO?

he discovery in China a few years ago of eggs found inside the body of a mother *Oviraptor* suggests that at least one type of theropod laid her eggs in a series of sittings like modern birds do, rather than all at once like crocodiles. The fossilized eggs were paired, so she probably laid them two at a time.

DID DINOSAURS SIT ON THEIR EGGS TO HATCH THEM?

f you weighed more than two fat hippos would you sit on your eggs? Not likely! Some duckbilled dinosaurs laid eggs in bowl-shaped mounds. Today most crocodiles and some birds do the same, covering their eggs with sand and plants. The dampness and warmth that build up inside the mound as the plants rot are perfect for incubating eggs. Large dinosaurs likely did the same because their eggs contained so many tiny pores that if they had been exposed to air they would have dried up inside. Recent research suggests that some smaller meat-eating theropods brooded their eggs in a very birdlike way.

◀ **This model of a *Protoceratops* baby hatching shows what a struggle it must have been for most dinosaurs to break out of their tough-shelled eggs.**

How LARGE WERE DINOSAUR EGGS?

I f you cracked open a nonfossilized *Hypselosaurus* egg, you could make scrambled eggs for 36 people. On the other hand, the smallest egg found to date contained a tiny *Mussaurus*. Its eggs were so small, they'd get lost in the bottom of your eggcup. In between were many sizes—and shapes. Both *Maiasaura* and *Hypacrosaurus* laid eggs about two-and-a-half times longer than a large chicken egg, but *Maiasaura's* eggs were lopsided ovals, while *Hypacrosaurus's* were ball-shaped.

A bird colony is a busy, noisy place at hatching time. Imagine what a dinosaur nesting ground must have been like.

▲ A paleontologist made this exact copy of a *Maiasaura* hatchling. The poorly formed joints of the original fossil told experts that this young dinosaur must have been quite helpless when it hatched.

▼ *Orodromeus* hatchlings were so well developed that they could run around as soon as they broke out of their eggs.

WERE BABY DINOSAURS HELPLESS WHEN THEY HATCHED?

ome were as helpless as newly hatched sparrows; others could run around as soon as they were out of the egg, like chickens can. Duckbill hatchlings, for instance, had poorly formed joints and bones. Their nests were full of trampled eggshells—proof that they spent a lot of time in them. Baby hypsilophodonts, however, had strong, fully formed bones and joints. Today their eggshells are found in one piece with just a hole in the top where the get-up-and-go hatchlings popped out and went.

DID BABY DINOSAURS CRAWL BEFORE THEY WALKED?

hen scientists looked inside a pair of 190 million-year-old eggs from South Africa they were delighted to find two perfectly formed *Massospondylus carinatus*, a long-necked plant-eater that walked on two legs. The shape of the babies' heads, necks and forearms suggest that they started life crawling on all fours. Possibly their large heads were too heavy for their necks to support—like yours when you were a baby.

▲ A dino-hunter works patiently to uncover a nest of *Protoceratops* eggs in the Gobi Desert. This parrot-beaked dinosaur laid 12 or more elongated eggs in a spiral, making sure that each egg stood upright.

 If your weight increased between birth and adulthood at the same rate as a duckbilled dinosaur's did, you'd weigh as much as four inter-city buses!

HOW BIG WAS A BABY DINOSAUR COMPARED WITH ITS PARENTS?

ow much did you weigh when you were born? By the time you're fully grown, you will have multiplied your birth weight by about 20 times. Newly hatched duckbilled dinosaurs were so tiny compared with their parents that they had to put on a 16,000-fold growth spurt to reach the same weight as their mom or dad.

DID DINOSAURS LOOK AFTER THEIR YOUNG?

These *Hypacrosaurus* hatchlings were the size of small poodles and completely helpless. One or both parents must have protected them and fed them berries and tender shoots. In China a *Psittacosaurus*, a small, plant-eating dinosaur, was found sitting on a nest of 34 youngsters! Some scientists think the adult was looking after several dinosaurs' young, just as Emperor penguins do so the adults can feed. And Montana's coyote-sized, two-legged, plant-eating *Oryctodromeus cubicularis* was a burrowing dinosaur. Its bones were found with those of two youngsters in a den at the end of a burrow...further proof that at least some dinosaurs looked after their young.

WHICH DINOSAUR WOULD MAKE THE BEST PET?

If your backyard was the same size as Central Park in New York, a small herd of *Apatosaurus* would be ideal. You'd need a lake and a year-round supply of fresh vegetation for them. But because they were used to a warm climate, you'd have to house them each winter in a building about half the length of a football field—which you'd have to keep clean! If all this sounds like too much work, perhaps one of the small carnivores, or meat-eaters, such as *Troodon* would be the right dino pet for you. Given *Troodon*'s speed, intelligence and appetite for small, warm, furry objects, though, it would be wise not to let it play with the neighbors' hamsters!

Like *Troodon*, the two most popular pets today are both small carnivores.

HOW MUCH WOULD IT **HURT** IF A PLANT-EATING DINOSAUR **BIT YOU?**

Being bitten by *Parasaurolophus* (right) would make you feel as if you'd stuck your hand in a blender. These dinosaurs didn't just have a single set of dentures. They had interlocking rows of teeth that formed a continuous grinding surface. First they'd bite; then they'd grind. Ouch!

IS IT TRUE THAT ONE SMALL DINOSAUR FOUGHT WITH KARATE KICKS?

 ot one, but several small meat-eating dinosaurs had a huge sickle-shaped claw on each back foot, which would have been deadly when used with a karate-like kick. *Velociraptor* from Mongolia was one; *Troodon* and *Deinonychus* from North America were two others. Some scientists think that *Deinonychus* hunted in packs. Part of the pack would grab hold of the victim's tail while the others delivered slashing kicks to the soft underbelly of their prey. You'll find a dynamic kick-boxing duo on page 29.

DID ANY BABY DINOSAURS HAVE BABY TEETH?

 aby hadrosaurs (duckbilled plant-eaters) have been found, still in their eggs, with tiny, perfectly formed baby teeth. Luckily, they didn't lose them all at once. Like all dinosaurs, hadrosaurs lost a tooth here and a tooth there and grew replacements for them all through their lives.

WHAT KIND OF TEMPERAMENT DID DINOSAURS HAVE?

las, it's impossible to tell from a bunch of old bones whether they held up a ferocious beast or a gentle creature. For all we know, *Mamenchisaurus* might have had a mean streak as long as its neck. Then again, it could have been as gentle as a lamb.

Parasaurolophus skull

Scientists nicknamed an African plant-eating sauropod with 600 teeth the Mesozoic Lawnmower.

WHICH WAS THE SMALLEST DINOSAUR?

Because birds are now known as avian (or flying) dinosaurs, one answer would be the bee hummingbird. (See page 56.) But dealing strictly with non-avian dinosaurs, the answer has to be *Microraptor*. This tiny dinosaur could stare a crow in the eye without having to bend down. Its body was covered in dinofuzz—long, wispy, partially formed feathers—and its feet look as if they could grasp branches. Who knows? *Microraptor* might have been the first tree-dwelling dinosaur.

ARE BLUE WHALES BIGGER THAN DINOSAURS?

Blue whales are the largest animals that have ever lived on Earth. Animals can grow bigger in the sea than they can on land because everything weighs less under water, just as it does in space. However, *Argentinosaurus*, a supersized South American sauropod, weighs in at 100 tons—about the same as a smallish blue whale. But if the largest blue whale flopped onto one side of the scales, about 26 T-rexes weighing a combined 160 tons would have to climb on the other side to balance it.

HOW BIG WAS APATOSAURUS'S INTESTINE?

When you're fully grown, your small intestine will be about 3 ½ times as long as you are tall. If *Apatosaurus* were the same, its small intestine would be 30 m (100 ft.) long. But scientists think it may actually have been 10 times that length. *Apatosaurus* needed a long intestine, and maybe even one with many large pouches. All that space was used to store its hard-to-digest plant food for extra-long periods of time so the bacteria inside could help to break the food down.

DID LONG-NECKED DINOSAURS GET NECK ACHE?

If the stretched-out sauropod *Mamenchisaurus* ever tried to board a school bus, its head would hit the back window before its front feet even got past the driver's seat. So it would be natural to think that sauropods like Big M would end up with a major case of sore neck muscles. However, chances are they didn't. Why? Because sauropod heads are very small in relation to their bodies and don't weigh much. (See how long you can comfortably hold an apple at arm's length then try it with a melon.) Their neck bones are lightweight too because they're filled with air spaces. And running along the top of the neck bones is a strong, rubber band-like ligament that acted a little like a bungee cord to support the neck in a horizontal position and take the load off neck muscles.

Compare a one-year-old baby with two *Mamenchisaurus* neck bones found in China. This sauropod had 19 neck bones (12 more than a giraffe). The smallest shown is 60 cm (2 ft.) long and the largest is 83 cm (2 ft. 9 in.) long.

What must it feel like to have a neck that measures half your entire stretched-out body length?

23

Is it true that some dinosaurs had two brains?

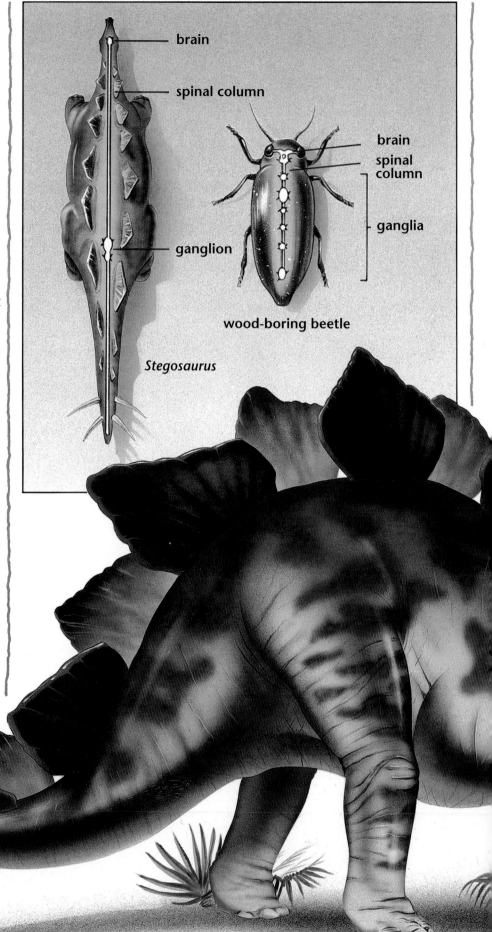

brain

spinal column

ganglion

Stegosaurus

brain

spinal column

ganglia

wood-boring beetle

Don't laugh. There's some truth to this rumor. What they had, however, wasn't so much a second brain as a large swelling of the spinal cord above their hips. The spinal cord is the thick bundle of nerves that connects the brain to every part of the body through a network of nerves. The swelling, or ganglion, acts like an automatic control center for parts of the body far away from the brain. It was especially important in large animals such as *Stegosaurus* that had to control huge back legs and use their tails as weapons.

All animals with backbones have this ganglion, and insects have many of them.

Stegosaurus

24

How SMART WERE DINOSAURS?

Would you describe a crocodile or an alligator as dim-witted? If so, you'd have to call most dinosaurs dim-witted, too, because they probably had as much brainpower as today's reptiles. Some of the small theropods—*Troodon*, *Oviraptor*, *Avimimus* and *Ornithomimus*—had larger-than-average dinosaur brains. It's thought that they were as smart as *Archaeopteryx*, the world's first bird. Now, if *Archaeopteryx* had the IQ of a chicken, that wouldn't have been much to boast about. But if it was as clever as a raven, then that would be something indeed.

IF I STEPPED ON A BIG DINOSAUR'S TAIL, HOW QUICKLY WOULD IT REACT?

Pain messages travel along nerves at speeds of 0.5 to 2 m (1 ½ to 6 ½ ft.) per second. *Seismosaurus*, a large, close relative of *Diplodocus*, is thought to have been about 32 m (105 ft.) long. If you stepped on *Seismosaurus*'s tail, it could take as long as 64 seconds before the message reached its brain. If *Seismosaurus* stepped on *your* toe, you'd say "Ouch!" much faster than that.

The small, carnivorous *Troodon* is considered by many paleontologists to be one of the smartest dinosaurs of them all.

HOW BIG WAS T-REX?

Tyrannosaurus rex was so tall that if you stood on a grown-up's shoulders, you would not even reach the level of its hips. T-rex was so long that it could bite the diving board in most backyard pools while hanging on to the wall at the shallow end with its tail. And T-rex was so heavy that if it climbed on one side of a seesaw, you'd have to balance the other side with 86 full-grown men!

WAS T-REX ALWAYS BIG?

Tyrannosaurs started out as small theropods covered in dinofuzz—a primitive type of feather. They remained small until, 15 million years before dinosaurs disappeared, T-rex grew into a giant and lost its feathers. Giants don't need feathers to keep warm.

T-REX: HUNTER OR SCAVENGER?

-rex's awesomely powerful bite drove its serrated banana-shaped teeth deep into bone, and plenty of fossils bear these marks. What's needed to prove that T-rex hunted for its dinner—maybe by ambushing its prey rather than chasing it—is a bone carrying tooth marks that had healed. That would mean T-rex ate fresh meat, not the equivalent of Cretaceous road kill. Or both, as some scientists believe.

If you ever came face to face with a T-rex, your screams would fall on deaf ears. It's likely that this monster could only detect sounds lower than the ones you make when you're scared out of your wits.

HOW LONG DID T-REX LIVE?

ue is the largest, most complete and oldest T-rex ever discovered. She survived to the not-very-old age of 28 despite back problems, broken ribs and many serious infections. This suggests to some researchers that other tyrannosaurs might have helped her when she was ill, possibly by bringing her food. A CT scan of her skull revealed that the part of her brain that handled the sense of smell was immense. Sue was a bloodhound among dinosaurs.

Tyrannosaurus rex skull

WAS T-REX REALLY THE KING OF DINOSAURS?

-rex would definitely have won the title of biggest, scariest meat-eating theropod in a North American competition. But at the world championships, 6-ton T-rex would take home the bronze. Patagonia's 8-ton *Gigantosaurus*

▲ **This skull belonged to "Black Beauty," a T-rex found in Alberta. (See page 15.)**

would claim the silver medal. And edging out Giganto for the gold, thanks to its extra 3 m (10 ft.) in length, would be the 8-ton super-brute *Spinosaurus*, a sail-backed monster representing North Africa. They might have been bigger, but T-rex still had the largest, deadliest teeth of them all.

▼ **T-rex was constantly growing sharp new teeth to take the place of the old ones it shed.**

27

WHICH WERE THE MOST FEROCIOUS DINOSAURS?

 magine a tag-wrestling match that pits the fiercest Cretaceous theropods against one another. You can decide the winners.

On this side are three super-heavyweights representing the land masses (originally Gondwana) that ended up in the southern hemisphere after Pangaea broke up (see page 38):

Super *Spinosaurus*

out of Africa. "Super S," the largest meat-eater on the planet, could clear any combat ring, providing it could fit inside. Avoid those crocodile-like jaws with interlocking teeth. Snap! And nothing escapes.

Gruesome *Gigantosaurus* ▼

from Argentina. Rumor has it that "Giganto" breaks trees in half to stay in shape. With a

brain half the size of T-rex's, "Giganto" might not be the sharpest fighter in the ring, but it's a real heavyweight contender with blade-like, slicing teeth.

Carnivorous *Carnotaurus*

from Patagonia. Opponents had better watch out when chilled-out "Carno" starts swinging its horns. Whatever you do, don't mention its short arms or this bull-headed dino might take offence. And you wouldn't want that to happen.

And on this side, representing the land masses (originally Laurasia) in the northern hemisphere are:

Treacherous ▲ *Troodon*

from Canada and the United States. This sharp-eyed fighter is one of the smartest around and specializes in lightning-fast rip-attacks. When the going gets slippery, "Treacherous T's" ribbed teeth are perfect for grabbing hold and hanging on.

Villainous ▶ *Velociraptor*

from China. It might be small, but "Villainous Velo" is one of the most powerful fighters around. Watch for its triple combination attack with teeth, hand and sickle claws, as well as its specialty: the double drop-kick.

◀ Terrible *Tyrannosaurus rex*

from Canada and the United States. "Born-to-Bite" T-rex earned its nickname the snappy way. Its jaws pack enough force to out-bite a modern alligator, driving nightmare teeth straight through bone and anything else that gets in the way.

▶ **Will the agility, speed and intelligence of the little guys in T-rex's corner make up for the sheer brute power of Super *Spinosaurus*'s gang? Only you can decide.**

The illustration below will help you pick out the shapes of *Protoceratops* and *Velociraptor* in this photograph. The battling pair were discovered in Mongolia by Polish paleontologists.

Protoceratops

Velociraptor

DID DINOSAURS EAT ONE ANOTHER?

When a team of Canadian and Chinese paleontologists found 12 young *Pinacosaurus* in the Gobi Desert (see pages 8 and 10), it was clear from teeth found at the scene that two theropods, *Velociraptor* and *Saurornithoides* had been feeding on them. *Velociraptor* had turned up before in the Gobi Desert, locked in combat with a horned dinosaur, *Protoceratops*. Whatever disaster overtook them both, *Velociraptor* was obviously not about to let go of a potential dinner.

It was once thought that dinosaurs never saw grass. Researchers now say the first grasses might have evolved 35 million years before dinosaurs disappeared.

DID MEAT-EATING DINOSAURS HUNT IN PACKS?

Scientists have found several skeletons of a new type of theropod named *Mapusaurus roseae* that obviously died together in a river flood. Who knows? Theropods that lived together might have hunted together. It would certainly make sense for a puny 8-ton *Gigantosaurus* to have back-up when it was stalking the 100-ton behemoth *Argentinasurus*. (See *Deinonychus*, page 21.)

► Leaf fossils offer clues about ancient climates. Large, tooth-edged leaves tell of cool, wet weather; small spiny ones of dry conditions. Long, slender leaves grew in windy spots, and smooth-edged ones with tips that let water drip grew in warm, damp places.

Monkey Puzzle

Cycad

Ginkgo

WHY DO SCIENTISTS COLLECT DINOSAUR DROPPINGS?

You can tell from the shape of dinosaur droppings, known as coprolites, what kind of dinosaur left them behind. Meat-eaters produced coil-shaped coprolites, like the one shown (left). Plant-munchers left shapeless piles of dung. Titanosaur dung has told scientists plenty about the environment in India 70 million years ago. It contained five species of grass, flowering plants, cycads and conifers. Not fussy eaters, then, titanosaurs.

Magnolia

English Laurel

Fern

Horsetail

Yew

DID DINOSAURS SIT DOWN TO EAT LOW BRANCHES OR VEGETATION?

Does a rhinoceros sit down to eat grass, or a giraffe squat to nibble on low branches? No, and for a good reason. A rhino's head is close to the ground because that is where all of its food grows. A giraffe's head is at the end of a long neck, so it can reach leaves on trees and bushes. Substitute *Triceratops* for the rhino and *Diplodocus* for the giraffe, and you can see how these two dinosaurs fed. And they'd have as little reason to sit down as the rhino and the giraffe do.

31

HOW CAN YOU TELL WHETHER A DINOSAUR ATE PLANTS OR MEAT?

Very occasionally, a dinosaur hunter will find a dinosaur whose stomach contents have been fossilized. Usually, however, they use other detective skills to determine dinosaur diets.

For instance, big mouths full of sharp teeth suggest that their owners attacked and ate other animals. If you went to the zoo at feeding time, you wouldn't expect to see lions and tigers munching on bales of hay.

On the other hand, mouths full of grinding teeth point to animals that had to chew tough vegetation. When was the last time you saw a cow with a wicked set of canines?

Even the shape and size of the dinosaur's body provide useful clues. A big head and jaws and a powerful, stocky neck belong on a meat-eater. And a long neck and small head belong to a plant-eater that browses on trees and bushes.

Try your sleuthing skills on these teeth and figure out whether they belong to a meat-eater (carnivore) or plant-eater (herbivore). But be careful. One set of teeth belongs to a dinosaur that scientists think might have eaten both meat and plants (an omnivore).

Massospondylus

had a mouth full of small, triangular, coarse-edged teeth that look as if they could either grip, slice or grind. These teeth belong to:
a. A carnivore. **b.** An herbivore.
c. An omnivore.

This relative of
Yangchuanosaurus

has sharp, serrated teeth that curve backward to give it a better grip on its meal. These teeth belong to:
a. A carnivore. **b.** An herbivore.
c. An omnivore.

Answers: page 64.

All of **Diplodocus's** ▶
pencil-like teeth are at the front of its
long, weak jaws. No good for chewing,
they were probably used for raking.
These teeth belong to:
a. A carnivore.
b. An herbivore.
c. An omnivore.

▼ **Edmontosaurus's**
battery of sharp, diamond-shaped teeth
act like a giant food grater to grind up
tough food. These teeth belong to:
a. A carnivore. **b.** An herbivore.
c. An omnivore.

◀ **Psittacosaurus**
didn't have many teeth, but its long,
sharp beak could slice easily through
tough, fibrous materials. These teeth belong to:
a. A carnivore. **b.** An herbivore. **c.** An omnivore.

HOW CAN YOU TELL MEAT-EATERS' AND PLANT-EATERS' FOOTPRINTS APART?

First check to see if the animal walked on two or four feet. Most meat-eating dinosaurs walked on two feet (*Baryonyx* was a possible exception) and left sharply pointed bird-like prints with three toes. Any dinosaur that walked around on four feet usually ate plants. However, some plant-eating duckbills and hypsilophodonts and some members of the pachycephalosaur and heterodontosaur families used two legs when it suited them.

No wonder the dinosaurs below look confused! The footprints they have left behind don't belong to them. Can you match up each dinosaur with its correct footprints?
Answers: page 64.

Elephants walk around on tiptoe. A shock-absorbing wedge of spongy tissue beneath each heel lifts them off the ground. Sauropods had the same type of spongy wedge beneath their heels.

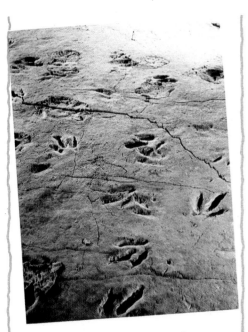

▲ **A cast of a duckbilled dinosaur footprint found in the Peace River Canyon, British Columbia.**

◀ **Tracks found in Connecticut's Dinosaur State Park resemble those made by *Dilophosaurus*.**

COULD DINOSAURS SWIM?

law scratches and footprints on old river and lake beds are the only evidence we have that some dinosaurs seem to have swum in shallow water where they occasionally touched bottom. Six pairs of S-shaped scratchmarks found in the bed of an ancient lake in northern Spain suggest that a large theropod had mastered the art of the dino-paddle. And tracks of only the front feet of a large sauropod can either mean it was very good at handstands or it was swimming with its rear end buoyed up by the water. In computer simulations of four types of sauropods in water, scientists discovered they could float, probably aided by their hollow neck bones. So these monster water babies likely used their front feet to punt their way through shallow water. Alas, as soon as the simulated sauropods got into deep water they rolled onto their sides like capsized boats.

The largest dinosaur footprint ever found belongs to a Chinese sauropod. At 1.5 m (5 ft.) long and 1.3 m (4 ft. 3 in.) wide, it's about the size of a child's wading pool.

CAN YOU TELL HOW FAST DINOSAURS MOVED?

ooster-sized *Compsognathus* was an Olympic sprinter—100 m (330 ft.) in just over six seconds! That's much faster than an adult T-rex. Some scientists claim that T-rex's leg bones weren't strong enough to support it at high speed. Others argue that T-rex might have been faster than its bones suggest because its flexible knees had thick pads of shock-absorbing cartilage—although a fall at high speed could have been fatal. Still others claim that to move fast, a 6-ton adult would have needed leg muscles totaling an impossible 86 percent of its body mass! One thing's certain. Whatever speed restrictions applied to T-rex also applied to its large prey.

Match the Movers

Paleontologists figured out how fast some well-known dinosaurs moved compared with some modern animals, but their results got jumbled up. Can you match up each animal with its correct speed?

Edmontosaurus	30 km/h (19 mph)
African elephant	67 km/h (42 mph)
Hypsilophodont	43 km/h (27 mph)
Tyrannosaurus rex	20 km/h (12 mph)
Racehorse	25 km/h (15 mph)
Coelurus	43 km/h (27 mph)
Ostrich	16 km/h (10 mph)

Answers: page 64.

DID YOUNG DINOSAURS STAY WITH THEIR PARENTS?

Paleontologists have found an enormous herd of duckbilled *Maiasaura* that were killed by a heavy fall of volcanic ash. The herd was made up of four distinct sizes of dinosaurs. Some scientists think that the two smallest sizes were babies and youngsters, and the two largest, teens and adults.

If this is so, *Maiasaura* grew up with the herd. The group of young *Pinacosaurus* that you met on page 8, however, appeared to have been traveling separately from their herd. No adult skeletons were found nearby. Of course, this could mean the youngsters were with a herd but were dawdling. It could also mean that any adults with them were able to dig themselves out after the sandstorm.

Even young *Pinacosaurus* had teeth, and the glove-shaped teeth of armored dinosaurs are unmistakable.

A "dinosaur highway" containing more than a million footprints of plant-eating dinosaurs was discovered running north-south along the eastern edge of the Rocky Mountains.

It is difficult to believe that the barren landscape of Bylot Island in the Canadian Arctic was once so full of plant life that dinosaurs found it a good place to live.

DID DINOSAURS MIGRATE?

n the summer of 1989 an expedition of Canadian and Chinese paleontologists went to Bylot Island in the Arctic in an attempt to solve the mystery of whether some dinosaurs migrated each year.

The team already knew that *Pachyrhinosaurus* remains had been discovered south of the Arctic, in Alaska and in northern and southern Alberta. If dinosaur fossils also could be found in the High Arctic, they would provide stronger evidence that dinosaurs migrated in search of food. Why? Even though the Arctic climate was milder then than it is now, Arctic winters were just as long and dark. Plants would become dormant for many months. How then could plant-eating dinosaurs survive unless they migrated south?

The expedition was a success. The remains of plant-eating *Pachyrhinosaurus* in the High Arctic makes it highly probable that they migrated south each autumn, to where the sun shone all winter and plants continued to grow. Herds of caribou do the same today.

A herd of *Maiasaura* desperately tries to outrun a rolling cloud of volcanic ash.

HOW DID DINOSAURS GET ALL OVER THE WORLD?

hen dinosaurs first evolved, they could have strolled from the Arctic to Antarctica without crossing a single sea. In those days, the Earth's seven continents were all joined together as one super landmass, Pangaea. But Pangaea began to split up about 150 million years ago and the continents started their slow drift apart. The same dinosaur families lived all over the world. After the continents split apart, southern hemisphere dinosaurs seemed caught in a Jurassic time warp. New species did evolve, but many remained relatively unchanged except in size—think *Spinosaurus*, the largest land predator of all time. In the north many more advanced forms evolved, including smaller, more intelligent dinosaurs such as *Troodon*.

70 million years ago, North America was divided by a great sea. A strip of land connected Western Canada and China.

Europe

North America

Africa

Asia

India

Australia

South America

Antarctica

ARE THE DINOSAURS OF NORTH AMERICA RELATED TO CHINESE DINOSAURS?

ou're a small dinosaur chomping on tasty plants in Wyoming 70 million years ago. You look up to see a *Tyrannosaurus rex* striding purposefully in your direction. How you wish you were far away in China. But don't be too hasty with those wishes! In China, you'd be just as likely to look up into the welcoming grin of a creature that could stand in as a movie double for T-rex. It's the deadly *Tarbosaurus bataar*.

Tyrannosaurus rex

If the continents drifted apart at the rate of only 10 cm (4 in.) a year, after 150 million years they'd have travelled 15,000 km (9,320 miles).

Scientists now know there's a whole other world of dinosaurs waiting to be discovered in the southern hemisphere. South America is the land of giants and Africa has already produced the hippo-like *Lurdusaurus* (below) with a wicked thumb claw and *Nigersaurus* (left), a small cousin of Diplodocus. This living lawnmower cropped ground vegetation with two rows of cutting teeth set along the straight edges of its spade-shaped mouth.

Are these two look-alikes related? They lived at a time when North America and Asia were joined together. (See map.) Almost all the dinosaur families found in North America at that time are also found in China. T-rex and T-bataar aren't exactly alike, but close enough to suggest strong family ties. Proof, perhaps, that dinosaurs moved between the two continents on land "bridges" that were exposed when sea levels fell.

Tarbosaurus bataar

DID ANY DINOSAURS HAVE A TRUNK?

lephant skulls have holes in the top for their noses. But their nostrils are at the end of a long trunk that sticks out of the front of their faces, not the top of their heads. Sauropods such as *Diplodocus* and *Brachiosaurus* had nose holes on top of their skulls too. Does this mean that they had trunks that grew from the front of their faces? We might never know. Noses, cheeks, lips and ears don't last long enough to fossilize. So go ahead and imagine *Brachiosaurus* with an enormous trunk or your favorite hadrosaur with floppy ears if you wish.

Little *Triceratops* hatched from their eggs looking quite round and cuddly—well, maybe their parents thought so. Fossils show that these dinosaurs didn't grow their impressive horns until they were young adults—between two and four years old.

WHAT USE WERE TRICERATOPS' HORNS AND FRILLS?

bviously, any T-rex would have thought twice before attacking T-top's sharp end. But there's a possibility that male *Triceratops* might also have locked horns in wrestling matches, like African antelope and bison do today. There's even a good chance the frill might have helped keep this huge plant-eater cool. How? As overheated blood traveled through the frill's many blood vessels it would radiate heat out into the air. An African elephant's large earflaps lose body heat in just the same way.

WHY DID SOME DUCKBILLED DINOSAURS HAVE CRESTS ON THEIR HEADS?

h, dear. You're a *Lambeosaurus* with a problem. You've got to choose a mate, but all the distinctive crests of the different types of duckbills that live close by are hidden. Can you pick out your *Lambeosaurus* mate from this group of dinosaurs?

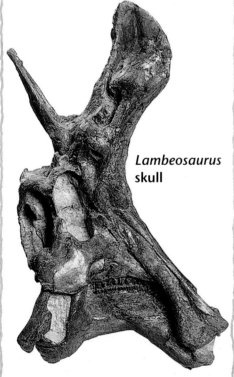

Lambeosaurus skull

You've seen how crests helped dinosaurs recognize others of their own species. But did you know that crests were also hollow? Each breath of air the dinosaur took went through the crest. Perhaps different-shaped crests produced different sounds. Their large size might even have increased the duckbills' sense of smell.

Without those telltale crests, it's not easy to find the *Lambeosaurus* mate. Now try again, below.

41

Here's what *Velociraptor* might have looked like with its warm coat of feathers.

WERE DINOSAURS WARM- OR COLD-BLOODED?

 warm-blooded tiger generates its own body heat from the large amounts of food it eats. It can be active whenever it wants. A cold-blooded snake, however, must absorb heat from the sun or its surroundings. It needs less food than a warm-blooded animal, but it can be active only if it stays warm.

Small, meat-eating dinosaurs were probably warm-blooded and therefore very active. But what about plant-eaters? The discovery of what appears to be a fossilized heart inside a plant-eating *Thescelosaurus*, nicknamed Willo, suggests that this pony-sized plant-eater might also have been warm-blooded. If the interpretation of a CT scan of the grapefruit-sized, rust-colored blob in Willo's chest is correct, its heart resembled a bird's or mammal's. This type of heart delivers oxygen more efficiently to the body than reptile hearts do—

what's needed to support an active, warm-blooded creature. It's possible that big dinosaurs were cold-blooded animals whose sheer bulk helped them stay warm. A leatherback turtle is a large, cold-blooded reptile that can store heat deep inside its body. When the turtle visits cold northern waters, the combination of its size and an insulating layer of blubber under the skin slows the escape of this stored heat to the surrounding water. If a one-ton turtle can stay warm in the cold, surely a dinosaur many times heavier could easily do the same? In fact, jumbo-sized dinos might even have suffered from overheating!

▶ **You can see the outline of feathers in the rock around this fossil of *Archaeopteryx*. (For more on *Archaeopteryx*, see page 56.)**

WHY DID SOME DINOSAURS HAVE FEATHERS?

The first dinosaur with a hint of feathers was discovered in China in 1996. Its body outline sported a fringe of feathery tendrils. After *Sinosauropteryx* hit the headlines, many more small feathered dinosaurs were found in China. Then in 2001, a young dromeosaur—a relative of *Velociraptor*, *Troodon* and *Archaeopteryx*—was found covered head to foot in fully formed feathers. None, however, were flight feathers. It would seem that small theropod dinosaurs grew feathers to keep themselves warm.

Dinofuzz and theropods' body feathers were terrific at keeping out the cold, but they were useless for getting dinosaurs airborne. Flight feathers must have a definite structure and shape, like the ones outlined in the rock around this fossil of *Archaeopteryx* (right), the oldest known avian dinosaur. (That's a bird to you.)

IS IT TRUE THAT SOME DINOSAURS HAD ARMOR?

If a *Tyrannosaurus rex* mom gave her offspring one piece of advice, it surely must have been, "Don't waste your time trying to bite a *Nodosaurus*." A researcher discovered that this armored dinosaur carried state-of-the-art body armor. Under a microscope, some of its protective plates were seen to be made up of strong fibers running in three different directions—the identical pattern, in fact, to that found in bullet-proof vests made out of Kevlar.

▼ This fossilized, tooth-breaking bony "scute" would have been one of many embedded in an armored dinosaur's skin.

WHAT COLOR WERE DINOSAURS?

 Scientists have found striped tail feathers on a turkey-sized *Caudipteryx* and a red and black, 70 million-year-old turtle shell. Unfortunately, color pigments usually disappear when skin becomes fossilized so dinosaur colors remain a mystery. But an Oxford University biologist has managed to reconstruct the color of ancient fish and beetles by examining structures—types of pigment cells—embedded in their fossils that produce color. Who knows? Fish today, dinosaurs tomorrow. Meanwhile, scientists look to modern animals for clues about color. Animals use color and patterns to attract a mate,

Albertosaurus

frighten off would-be attackers or camouflage themselves.

Here's how four types of familiar animals camouflage themselves. The illustrations show how dinosaurs would have looked if they had done the same.

Spots and Stripes

Leopards and tigers have patterned coats that make them difficult to see against the contrasting light and shade of their forest surroundings. Dinosaurs that lived in similar settings might have had similar patterns and colors.

Dark and Light ▶

Have you noticed how many animals—ranging from killer whales to antelopes and hawks—have a dark back and a pale belly? Land animals with this kind of shading are difficult to see against bright open spaces. The same would apply to small dinosaurs living in similar conditions.

Orodromeus

Invisible Babies

Cougars give birth to spotted babies, and wild boar babies are born with stripes. When these babies remain still on the forest floor, their spots and stripes make them almost invisible. Think how much safer a spotted or striped baby dinosaur would have been if it too lived in a forest. ▶

Parasaurolophus

Brachiosaurus

Too Big to Care

Many big African animals—elephants, rhinos, hippos and crocodiles—are gray all over. They don't need camouflage patterns or color. They rely on their horns, teeth and bulk for protection. Sauropods probably relied on their size and were likely as drab and gray as elephants and rhinos.

HOW BIG COULD A DINOSAUR GET?

I f you could magically grow bigger, until you had twice as much skin (what scientists call your surface area), you would find that you weighed far more than twice as much as you used to. If you continued to grow, your weight would increase faster than the strength of the body parts that hold you together. If you grew too big your weight would eventually crush your leg bones. As strange as it seems, the bigger you get, the weaker you get. This is probably why dinosaurs never got any bigger than *Argentinosaurus*—weighing as much as 18 African elephants and only 10 m (33 ft.) shorter in length than an Olympic-size swimming pool, making it the largest animal that ever walked the Earth.

Only fragments of *Argentinosaurus* have been found but "Ultrasaurus" is one of the largest dinosaurs ever excavated. If it stood on tiptoe, it could peek through the sixth-floor windows in an apartment building. From its nose to the tip of its tail it was as long as three school buses, and it weighed more than 15 African elephants.

◀ **James Jensen standing beside the colossal front leg of "Ultrasaurus," a huge dinosaur that he discovered in Colorado in 1979.**

HOW DO WE KNOW DINOSAURS DIDN'T LIVE BEYOND 65 MILLION YEARS AGO?

n Alberta's badlands, and other places around the world, are layers of rock that are between 65 million and 90 million years old. These layers are full of dinosaur fossils. In the newer rocks immediately above the 65-million-year-old layer, you will find only the skeletons of reptiles and many mammals, but no dinosaur skeletons.

In a few places around the world, single dinosaur bones have been found in rocks less than 65 million years old. And at some sites, *Triceratops* teeth have also been dug out of newer rock. But many scientists think that these dinosaur fossils didn't really belong in the newer rocks. It's likely that they got washed out of older levels and were then reburied among newer material.

IF DINOSAURS WERE SO BIG AND STRONG, WHY DID THEY BECOME EXTINCT?

t doesn't matter whether you're as small as a water snail or as big and powerful as a polar bear. It doesn't even matter whether you're intelligent or not, fast or slow, warm-

▲ **65 million years ago, Alberta's Horseshoe Canyon was a sandy delta surrounded by swamp. The sandy areas show up as thick light layers, the swamp as dark bands of coal.**

blooded or cold-blooded. Survival of a species has to do with how well all its members can adapt to changes in their environment so that they can go on producing offspring. Dinosaurs obviously weren't flexible enough to adapt to the mysterious changes that swept the Earth 65 million years ago.

Triceratops

WHICH DINOSAURS WERE THE FIRST TO BECOME EXTINCT?

Dinosaurs began to die out soon after they first appeared more than 200 million years ago. They didn't all wait until 65 million years ago to become suddenly extinct.

The dinosaurs at the top of the page are some of the earliest to evolve and, therefore, among the first to become extinct. As the dinosaurs in each group died out, new ones evolved to take their place. Each step down the page contains more recent dinosaurs. Did *Apatosaurus* ever meet *Tyrannosaurus rex*?

Apatosaurus couldn't have met *Tyrannosaurus rex* because it became extinct 70 million years before T-rex came along. In fact, you live closer in time to T-rex than *Apatosaurus* ever did!

Dinosaurs that became extinct 200 million years ago

Dinosaurs that became extinct 175 million years ago

Dinosaurs that became extinct 135 million years ago

Dinosaurs that became extinct 90 million years ago

Dinosaurs that became extinct 65 million years ago

Staurikosaurus

Scedlidosaurus

Mamenchisaurus

Brachiosaurus

Nemegtosaurus

Massospondylus   *Procompsognathus*   *Herrarasaurus*   *Coelphysis*

Dilophosaurus   *Vulcanodon*   *Segisaurus*   *Lesothosaurus*

Allosaurus   *Stegosaurus*   *Yangchuanosaurus*   *Apatosaurus*

Psittacosaurus   *Iguanadon*   *Wuerhosaurus*   "Sinornithoides"

Thescelosaurus   *Tyrannosaurus rex*   *Leptoceratops*   *Triceratops*

49

DID SOMETHING FROM SPACE KILL THE DINOSAURS?

ixty-five million years ago, 70 percent of all animal species ceased to exist and a thin layer of iridium was deposited all over the world. This mineral is rare on the Earth's surface but plentiful deep inside the planet and in comets and meteorites.

Many scientists think that the iridium came from a 10 km- (6 mile-) wide comet or meteorite strike 65 million years ago. The impact would blast vast amounts of pulverized rock out of the atmosphere, some halfway to the Moon. Friction caused by the dust and debris falling back to Earth would heat the air to the point where whole continents burst into flame. Large animals, unable to find refuge from the terrible firestorm, would perish.

After the sky cooled, dust would block the sun's light, plunging the world into an "impact winter" lasting many years, probably followed by global warming as carbon dioxide levels rose. Animal species that failed to adapt to these extreme conditions died out. Amazingly, 30 percent of all animal species managed to survive.

▶ (right) A comet approaches Earth.

▶ (opposite) Ten seconds after impact. Vaporized rock and water rise 100 km (60 miles) into the atmosphere.

DID VOLCANOES CAUSE THE DEATH OF THE DINOSAURS?

ecently discovered fossil evidence suggests that massive volcanic eruptions in India causing lava flows 2 km (1 1/4 miles) thick also happened 65 million years ago. If enough volcanoes spewed lava and ash into the air at the same time, they would have the same effect as the impact of a giant meteor. All of the resulting dust, chemicals, gas and ash would cause significant changes in the Earth's climate.

A new idea is that a gigantic underground explosion called a Verneshot might have been responsible for the mass extinctions at the end of the Cretaceous period. It would bring iridium to the surface from deep inside the Earth and it would produce a gigantic crater full of the same kind of shocked and melted rock found at the site of a meteor impact. Yet another hot topic for debate.

WHERE ON EARTH IS THE METEORITE CRATER?

A meteorite 10 km (6 miles) across would leave a crater 150 km (93 miles) across. How could we miss something this big? It might have been buried under floods of lava, or it could be on the sea floor. Scientists think that the Chicxulub crater at the tip of Mexico's Yucatán Peninsula fits the bill.

▲ Arizona's Meteor Crater is a mere 49,500 years old and 1.2 km (³/4 mile) across.

HOW COULD ONE DISASTER KILL ALL THE DINOSAURS?

M aybe a combination of events caused the mass extinctions 65 million years ago: there's evidence that species were disappearing long before the meteorite strike. One theory is that the Earth passed through a gigantic cloud of dust and gas, which cooled the planet, killing off species that couldn't adapt to climate change. The immense gravity of the cloud may also have affected the path of comets. One of these could have struck Earth—and the rest you know.

51

IS IT POSSIBLE TO CLONE A DINOSAUR?

To clone an animal you use the living contents of one of its cells—its DNA—to produce an exact replica of the original animal. When an animal dies and becomes fossilized, all its DNA usually gets fossilized, too, and then it can't be used for cloning. Some scientists think there is an extremely remote chance, however, that a dinosaur might be found in such a good state of preservation that its DNA could be reconstructed to produce a clone.

If birds have dinosaur DNA, altered by millions of years of evolution, could scientists rewind evolution by recreating dinosaur genes out of bird DNA? Already, researchers have come up with ancient genes that give chickens back the teeth they lost 60 million years ago.

IS THE LEGEND OF A DINOSAUR IN AFRICA BASED ON A TRUE CREATURE?

 Mokele-mbembe is described as a hippo-size, sauropod-type creature that lives in the river systems of northern Congo and southern Chad and feeds on malombo fruit, also known as jungle chocolate. However, there is no proof that this shy, sweet-toothed vegetarian is a real animal, let alone a dinosaur. Paleontologists think Mokele-mbembe stands as much chance of being a dinosaur as it does of being an extraterrestrial.

WHAT WOULD HAVE HAPPENED TO THE DINOSAURS IF THEY HADN'T DIED OUT?

 During the last few million years of the dinosaurs' existence, a small, swift theropod called *Troodon* evolved. It came from an old family of large-brained dinosaurs. *Troodon* ran around on two legs and had three digits on its hands, one of which it could use like a thumb to grasp things. Its eyes were huge. They were also forward-facing, giving *Troodon* good depth perception for

▲ Crocodiles haven't changed much since the time of dinosaurs. If *Troodon* had changed as little, it would look today just as it did 65 million years ago.

hunting. It's possible that this creature wouldn't have evolved much at all. But the model, opposite, shows what paleontologist Dale Russell thinks *Troodon* might have evolved into if dinosaurs hadn't become extinct.

WHICH ANIMALS HAVE **CHANGED** THE **LEAST** SINCE DINOSAUR TIMES?

Welcome to a hot, humid Jurassic swamp 160 million years ago. The animals here, with the exception of the pterosaur, have descendants living today. Some have changed little since Jurassic times, but one might surprise you. Can you match up each animal with its description?

Answers: page 64.

Animal Descriptions

1. Salamanders haven't changed much, and even this ancient one had bright colors.

2. *Archaeopteryx* was a tiny theropod with wings and feathers.

3. Each of *Rhamphorhynchus*'s wings was supported by an enormously long feather.

4. Beetles, like this predatory ground beetle, were very common all through the age of reptiles.

5. This swamp-dwelling crocodile could grow as long as 6 m (20 ft.).

6. This turtle couldn't pull its head into its shell.

7. This 7 cm- (2 ³/₄ in.-) long katydid looked a lot like its living relatives, and even more like a green leaf.

8. This dragonfly had a wingspan of about 20 cm (8 in.) and hunted smaller insects.

9. This ancestor of the snake had short legs.

10. This cat-sized mammal, called *Triconodon*, probably laid eggs like a reptile but nursed its young like other mammals.

11. This frog lived mostly on land and was a powerful jumper.

12. This tuatara—the only survivor of an ancient group of reptiles called sphenodontids—ate insects and worms.

IS IT REALLY TRUE THAT BIRDS ARE DINOSAURS?

 ext time you stock up your bird feeder, pat yourself on the back for helping to keep a long line of singing dinosaurs alive and flapping. According to the way scientists now classify animals, all the descendants of a particular ancestor are grouped under the same name. Since birds and dinosaurs descended from one particular dinosaur ancestor, they're all dinosaurs. You'll have already noticed that scientists now speak about avian dinosaurs (birds) and non-avian dinosaurs (dinosaurs).

DID ALL DINOSAURS TURN INTO BIRDS?

 nly one type of dinosaur evolved into birds: an unknown small, meat-eating, feathered theropod. All theropods had birdlike bodies. You can easily see this in *Velociraptor* or *Troodon*. You have to look hard to see it in *Tyrannosaurus*, but it's true. Tests done on soft tissue found in a T-rex thigh bone reveal that its collagen—the protein that gives bone its structure—is almost identical in its makeup to that of a chicken! Think of that the next time you gnaw on a drumstick.

► Here is one artist's impression of how dinosaurs evolved into birds.

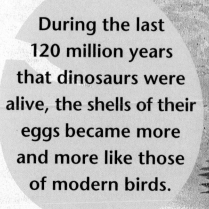

WAS ARCHAEOPTERYX THE FIRST BIRD?

 rchaeopteryx fossils appeared 10 million years after dinosaurs began to develop birdlike features. *Archaeopteryx* still had a dinosaur tail and weapon-like claw (like a mini-*Velociraptor*), but it had developed wings, flight feathers and a birdlike brain well suited for flight. That's why many think that *Archaeopteryx* is the world's first bird. But there are always new discoveries. For instance, bird-like footprints 55 million years older than Archae have recently been discovered in Argentina.

WERE THERE ANY BIG FEATHERED DINOSAURS?

 es. The bird-like predator *Gigantoraptor erlianensis*, which lived in China about 70 million years ago, stood as tall as T-rex and weighed as much as a hippo. Scientists were shocked when they found it. No wonder. That's one scary-sounding bird.

During the last 120 million years that dinosaurs were alive, the shells of their eggs became more and more like those of modern birds.

WHY DID MAMMALS ONLY GET BIG AFTER THE DINOSAURS BECAME EXTINCT?

T hings balance out well in nature. There is only room for a certain number of big predators and plant-eaters. Unfortunately for mammals, dinosaurs occupied all these positions for 150 million years. As soon as the dinosaurs became extinct, however, mammals were able to take advantage of the territories and food that the dinosaurs no longer needed. The many new species of mammals that arose gradually grew bigger and stronger.

In this scene, you'll find five dinosaurs and five mammals. Can you figure out which mammals took the place of which dinosaurs?

Answers: page 64.

Some mammals were big and bold enough to go dinosaur hunting. One mammal, about the size of a really big house cat, was found with a belly full of bones from a young *Psittacosaurus*.

Hypacrosaurus

Deinonychus

Brachiosaurus

Orodromeus

Tyrannosaurus rex

WHERE WERE PEOPLE DURING THE DINOSAUR AGE?

t's difficult to imagine the world without people, yet it got by until very recently without us. To give you an idea of just how new people are, imagine you're reading a book about the history of life on Earth. This heavy book has 1000 pages and covers a span of 3 ½ billion years. The human race—*Homo sapiens*—gets its first mention in the last couple of lines on the very last page, long after you finish reading about the life of the dinosaurs.

People, or *Homo sapiens*, hadn't evolved when dinosaurs were around, but your distant ancestors, the first primates, appeared late in the dinosaur age. Today the dinosaurs are gone, but the primates have remained. Remarkably, one species of primate developed enough brainpower to be able to look back over millions of years and prove that a successful race of super-reptiles once roamed the Earth. The likes of the dinosaurs had never been seen before and will never be seen again. But of the millions of species that live on Earth today, only yours knows of the dinosaurs' existence— and what an existence it was.

Glossary

Dinosaurs have some of the most awkward names ever invented. But successfully wrapping your tongue around a difficult dinosaur name is half the fun of getting to know them. Besides, you can really impress people by how fast you can rattle off *Micropachycephalosaurus* (remember it from page 6?).

On these pages, you'll find all the Latin and Greek words that make up the names of the dinosaurs and some of the other animals in this book.

First you'll see the word, then its origin or the language it comes from, followed by its meaning.

If you want to know what *Protoceratops* means, look down the list until you come to a word beginning with the letters *pro*. You'll find the meaning of *proto*. Next, look for *cerat* and add its meaning onto the first part. All that's missing now is the *ops*. Put the three parts together and you get a dinosaur name that means: "first-horned-face" (*proto-cerat-ops*).

All the names here either describe what dinosaurs look like or do, or the place where they were discovered, or occasionally the person who discovered them.

Names of dinosaurs and other creatures

Name	Origin	Meaning	Name	Origin	Meaning
A			**D**		
alberto	place name	Alberta, Canada	*deino, dino*	Greek	terrible (awesome)
allo	Greek	different	*delta*	Greek	delta
anchi	Greek	near	*di*	Greek	two
ankylo	Greek	crooked	*di*	Chinese	emperor
anuro	Greek	without a tail	*diplo*	Greek	twofold
apato	Greek	lying, deceitful	*docus*	Greek	beam
archaeo, archo	Greek	very old	*don, dont,*		
argentino	place name	Argentina	*donto*	Greek	tooth
avi, avis	Latin	bird	*dromeus*	Greek	runner
B			**E**		
bary	Greek	heavy	*edmonto*	place name	Edmonton, Canada
bataar	Mongolian	hero	*elasmo*	Greek	metal plate
brachio	Greek	arm	*ensis*	Latin	place, country, locality
C			*erlian*	place name	Erlian, Mongolia
carinatus	Latin	having a keel	**G**		
carno	Latin	meat-eating	*gallus, galli*	Latin	chicken, rooster
centro	Greek	point, midpoint	*giganto*	Greek	giant
cephalo	Greek	head	*gnathus*	Greek	jaw
cerat, ceros	Greek	horn			
cetio	Greek	monstrous	**H**		
coelo	Greek	hollow	*hadro*	Greek	large, strong
compso	Greek	elegant, pretty	*herrera*	place name	Herrera, Argentina
cono	Greek	cone	*hetero*	Greek	other, different
copro	Greek	dung, excrement	*hongtuyan*	Mandarin	red rocks
corytho	Greek	helmet	*hypacro*	Greek	below the top
cubicularis	Latin	of the lair	*hypselo, hypsi*	Greek	high
			I		
			ichthyo	Greek	fish
			iguano	Caribbean	iguana lizard

Name	Origin	Meaning
L		
lambe,		
lambeo	person's name	Lawrence Lambe
lepto	Greek	delicate
lesotho	place name	Lesotho, Africa
lestes	Greek	robber, pirate
lites	Greek	stone
long	Chinese	dragon
lopho	Greek	crest, ridge
lurdu	Latin	heavy
M		
maia	Greek	good mother
mamenchi	place name	Mamenchi, China
mapu	Mapuche	of the earth
masso	Greek	elongated
mega, megalo	Greek	great, big
micro	Greek	small
mimus	Greek	imitate, mimic
morpho	Greek	shape
multi	Latin	many
mus	Latin	mouse
N		
nemegt	place name	rock layer in Asia
niger	place name	Niger, Africa
nodo	Latin	knob
nychus	Greek	claw
O		
oides	Greek	like
onto	Greek	being, thing
onyx, onychus	Greek	claw
ops	Greek	face
ornith, ornitho	Greek	bird
oro	Greek	mountain
orycto	Greek	digging
ovi	Latin	egg
P		
pachy	Greek	thick
para	Greek	beside
physis	Greek	condition, nature
pilosus	Greek	hair
pinaco	Greek	board, plank
plesio	Greek	near, recent
pod	Greek	foot
pro	Greek	before
proto	Greek	first
psittaco	Greek	parrot
ptero, pteryx	Greek	wing, feather
R		
raptor	Latin	grabbing
rex	Latin	king
rhampho	Greek	curved beak
rhino	Greek	nose
rhynchus	Greek	snout
roseae	Latin/ person's name	rose color; also Rose Letwin
S		
saur, saura,		
sauro, saurus	Greek	reptile
scelido	Greek	limb
segi	place name	Segi Canyon, Arizona
segno	Latin	slow
seismo	Greek	earth shaking
sino	Latin	China
sordes	Latin	dirt, filth
spino	Latin	thorn, spine
spondylus	Greek	vertebra (backbone)
stauriko	Greek	cross
stego	Greek	roof
T		
tarbo	Greek	frightful
theco	Greek	sheath
thero	Greek	summer
thescelo	Greek	wonderful
tri	Greek	three
troo	Greek	wounding
tsintao	place name	Tsintao (Qingdao), China
tyranno	Greek	tyrant
U		
ultra	Latin	beyond
urus	Greek	tail
V		
veloci	Latin	swift, speedy
volcano	Latin	volcano
W		
wuerho	place name	Wuerho, China
Y		
yangchuan,		
yangchuano	place name	Yangchüan, China

Dinosaur Terms

archosaurs   The "ruling reptile" group that consisted of dinosaurs, pterosaurs, crocodilians, birds and their thecodont ancestors.

Cretaceous   The period between 65 million and 144 million years ago, from the Latin word *creta*, meaning chalky. Shallow, warm seas were common during this time, and chalky layers of rock accumulated on their floors.

hadrosaurs   Large, duckbilled plant-eaters that walked on two or four feet.

hypsilophodonts   Medium-size plant-eaters that walked on two feet. They looked like small hadrosaurs, but they weren't duckbilled.

Jurassic   The period between 144 million and 213 million years ago, named for the rocks laid down in the Jura Mountains of France and Switzerland; a time when the super-continent of Pangaea was splitting into two major landmasses.

Ornithischia   One of the two great groups of dinosaurs (*see also* Saurischia), which included plant-eating dinosaurs with horny beaks and leaf-shaped crowns on their teeth. Also known as bird-hipped dinosaurs.

paleontologist   A scientist who specializes in the study of ancient life on Earth.

plesiosaurs   Marine reptiles (not dinosaurs) with paddle-like feet and sharp teeth for eating fish. Some had long necks; others had short necks.

pterosaurs   Flying reptiles (not dinosaurs) with skin wings supported by one very long finger. The smallest ones were sparrow-size; the largest ones were the size of a small airplane.

Saurischia   The second of the two great groups of dinosaurs (*see also* Ornithischia), which included two-legged meat-eating theropods and mainly four-legged plant-eating sauropods. Also known as lizard-hipped dinosaurs.

sauropods   Very large, four-legged plant-eaters with long necks and small heads. Their backbones were often hollowed out to reduce their weight, and their long tails balanced their necks.

thecodonts   Most were four-legged reptiles (not dinosaurs) that were the ancestors and cousins of dinosaurs, pterosaurs and crocodilians.

theropods   Two-legged meat-eating dinosaurs with bird-like bodies. Most had sharp teeth and clawed fingers.

Triassic   The period between 213 million and 248 million years ago, during which three successive layers of rocks were laid down in Germany. During this time, Pangaea was showing its first signs of splitting up.

Index

Answers

Are you a Dino-Buff? (page 4)
1. b. Dinosaurs belonged to a group of "ruling reptiles" called Archosauria.
2. c. One of the earliest known dinosaurs, *Herrerasaurus*, lived in South America.
3. a.
4. b.
5. b. Ocean creatures such as *Elasmosaurus* and other plesiosaurs may have looked like dinosaurs, but they were a different kind of reptile.
6. c.
7. c. Dinosaurs, crocodilians, pterosaurs, birds and their thecodont ancestors formed the "ruling reptile" group.
8. a.
9. a. Meat-eaters (theropods) and long-necked plant-eaters (sauropods) were lizard-hipped dinosaurs. All other plant-eaters were bird-hipped.
10. b.
11. a.
12. c. The name dinosaur was invented in 1842 by British scientist Richard Owen. Of course, we now know that they were reptiles, but not lizards.

Dinosaur Jumble (page 6)

tri: three	micro: small
dino: terrible	tyranno: tyrant
mega: big	donto: tooth
pod: foot	saur: reptile

Check out the glossary on pages 60–63 for more unusual names.

Paleontologists' Tools (page 10)

1. tape measure	6. magnifying glass
2. jackhammer	7. air scribe
3. camera	8. burlap
4. brush	9. geological hammer
5. glue	10. rope and pulleys

Plant-eaters or Meat-eaters? (page 32)

Massospondylus: c.	*Edmontosaurus*: b.
Yangchuanosaurus: a.	*Psittacosaurus*: b.
Diplodocus: b.	

Footprint Mix-up (page 34)
A: 2, B: 3, C:4, D:1

Match the Movers (page 35)

Edmontosaurus: 20 km/h (12 mph)	Racehorse: 67 km/h (42 mph)
African elephant: 30 km/h (19 mph)	*Coelurus*: 43 km/h (27 mph)
Hypsilophodont: 16 km/h (10 mph)	Ostrich: 43 km/h (27 mph)
Tyrannosaurus rex: 25 km/h (15 mph)	

Animals from Dinosaur Times (page 54)
All the animals except *Rhamphorthynchus* (C) survived to the present day. Did you identify the crocodile (B), tuatara (F), ground beetle (G), turtle (H), frog (I), salamander (J), katydid (K) and dragonfly (L) as animals that have hardly changed at all in 160 million years? And *Archaeopteryx* (A), apart from its teeth and the claws on its wings, is recognizable as a bird. The cat-size mammal, *Triconodon* (D), may have been an ancient ancestor of today's Monotremata—duckbilled platypuses and prickly echidnas. And the lizard (E) might surprise you: it's an ancestor of the snake.

Present-Day Mammals (page 58)
Large predators such as polar bears took the place of big theropods such as *Tyrannosaurus rex*. Smaller predators such as wolves took the place of small theropods such as *Deinonychus*. Big plant-eaters such as elephants took the place of *Brachiosaurus* and other sauropods. Antelopes took the place of *Orodromeus* and other hypsilophodonts, and cows took the place of *Hypacrosaurus* and other hadrosaurs.

Credits

Photography Credits
pages 3 (background), 7, 10, 18 Brian Noble; 7 (inset) R.L. Christie; 6, 9, 14 (upper), 37 Mike Todor; 11 (camera) Nikon D3 Digital SLR with AF-S Zoom NIKKOR 24-70mm f/2.8G IF ED; 12 Peter Menzel/Science Photo Library; 13 Steve Allen/Science Photo Library; 14 (lower) Alan Bibby/Great North Communications; 36 John Acorn.

The following copyrighted photographs were used with permission of the individual or institution indicated in each case: page 30 Wojciech Skarzynski, courtesy of the Institute of Paleobiology, Polish Academy of Sciences, Warsaw; 35 courtesy of Dinosaur State Park, Rocky Hill, Connecticut; 17 Donald Baird (reconstruction by J. R. Horner); 43 Smithsonian Institution, photo No. 856814; 46 © by Mark A. Philbrick, Brigham Young University; 47 Royal Tyrrell Museum/Alberta Culture and Multiculturalism; 51 courtesy of Meteor Crater, Northern Arizona.

All other photographs by Kate Kunz.

Our thanks to the Royal Tyrrell Museum of Palaeontology for permission to photograph the following items from their collection: pages 10–11, paleontology tools; 3, 14–15, cast of *Mamenchisaurus* skeleton; 15, "Black Beauty" bones; 21, *Parasaurolophus* skull; 27, "Black Beauty" skull, *Tyrannosaurus rex* tooth; 31, dinosaur coprolite; 32–33, skulls of *Diplodocus*, *Edmontosaurus*, *Massospondylus*, *Psittacosaurus* and relative of *Yangchuanosaurus*; 35, cast of duckbilled dinosaur footprint; 41, *Lambeosaurus* skull; 44, ankylosaurid scute.

Our thanks to the Institute of Vertebrate Paleontology and Paleo-anthropology, China, for permission to photograph the following items from their collection: page 36, small fossilized *Pinacosaurus*.

Illustration Credits
pages 6–7 Dan Hobbs; 8–9 Steve Pilcher; 12 Joe Tucciarone/Science Photo Library; 16 "Protoceratops" model © by Sylvia Czerkas; 17 "Orodromeus Nesting Site (Egg Mountain)" © by Douglas Henderson; 19 "Hypacrosaurus Feeding Young" © by John Gurche; 20–21 Dan Hobbs; 22–23 "Mamenchisaurus Crossing the Flats" © 1986 by Mark Hallett; 23 Graeme Walker and Claudia Dávila; 24 Graeme Walker; 24–25 Graeme Walker; 25 Dan Hobbs; 26 Roger Harris/Science Photo Library; 28, 29 Grame Walker; 30 "A Fight to the Death" © 1984 by Mark Hallett with permission of the Natural Wildlife Federation; 31 Graeme Walker; 34 Dan Hobbs; 36–37 © by Doug Henderson, collection of the Museum of the Rockies; 38, 39 Graeme Walker; 40 Dan Hobbs; 41 Dan Hobbs; 42 Steve Pilcher; 44, 45 Graeme Walker; 47 "Triceratops" model © by S. & S. Czerkas; 48–49 Graeme Walker; 50–51 "Extinction of Dinosaurs" by Eleanor M. Kish, reproduced with permission of the Canadian Museum of Nature, Ottawa; 52 "Troodon" by Ron Séguin in collaboration with Dr. Dale Russell, reproduced with permission of the Canadian Museum of Nature, Ottawa; 53 "Dinosaurid" by Ron Séguin in collaboration with Dr. Dale Russell, reproduced with permission of the Canadian Museum of Nature, Ottawa; 54–55 Steve Pilcher; 56–57 "Dinosaur into Bird" © 1985 by Mark Hallett; 58, 59 Graeme Walker.